PEARLS OF GREAT PRICE

Pearls of Great Price

MARY ANN SULLIVAN

Purelilly Press

First Printing, 2024

ISBN: 979-8-9879-012-4-3

Published by Purelilly Press Publishing
Huntsville, Texas

Unless otherwise noted, Scripture quotations are from the King James Version. Quotations identified NKJV are from the New King James Version, copyright © 1979, 1980, 1982, Thomas Nelson, Inc., Publishers. Quotations identified NIV are from the Holy Bible, New International Version, copyright © 1973, 1978, 1984 by International Bible Society. Quotations identified CSV are from the Holy Bible, Christian Standard Bible, copyright © 2017 by Holman Bible Publishers. Quotations identified ASV are from the Holy Bible, American Standard Version, which is in the public domain, and quotes are obtained from BibleGateway.com. All uses of italic in biblical text has been added by the author for emphasis.

Contents

Prologue

I wish for you to walk with me on my journey with the Lord. The writings found within these pages are from times when the Lord taught me great wisdom and, more importantly, gave me profound revelations of his love and his heart.

At the end of this journey, my prayer is that you will have a deeper appreciation of and for God, our heavenly Father, Jesus, his son and our redeemer, and the Holy Spirit, our comforter and counselor in life.

Every journey is its own experience. Some are happy, some are sad. Some are long, and some are short. But when you allow Jesus to go with you, it is the experience of a lifetime!

I have gained wisdom and knowledge. I have experienced joy and sorrow. I have fallen, and I have soared. Through my journey, I have learned treasured lessons, and now I share them with you.

My Pearls of Great Price!

Chapter 1

He's Speaking...
Listen!

The time I have spent with my father I have found to be the most loving, comforting, peaceful, and yes, correcting time of my life. When I wander off from his presence as we all do at times, there is a loneliness and sense of loss beyond description. But the wonderful thing about my father is that he knows where I am, and he always comes to get me, be it with the whisper of my name or a hand that snatches me quickly from impending danger. Fathers are just like that! They can see to where you have not yet been. Fathers will lovingly and sternly set your feet on the right path.

Right about now you may be thinking, "Well, that doesn't sound anything like my father." The truth is it doesn't sound like my earthly father. The father I'm talking about is my heavenly father, and until you've been touched by his love, you've not been touched. I would like to share some of the things he has said to me. Hopefully, my experiences will cause you to hunger for a relationship of your own with him. Never think for one moment that God doesn't talk because he does. Never think that he will talk to me but will not talk to you, because that thought is just not true. Yes, he may speak to you differently because we are all different people, but let me assure you, he will speak if you listen.

Some of the things I want to share with you may be hard for you to believe but I promise you they are true. It has been a journey of the spirit; exciting, happy, and sometimes sad and sobering. I can promise you there is no journey like the one you will take with "Daddy God." After experiencing mine, I pray you will seek one of your own. It will be a and because there is no end to God or the journey he wants to take you on. You are in rehearsal now for what will never end. I pray you are listening to the Master of the Ages.

The Holy Spirit spoke to me in my spirit, "Your mission is to teach the heart of humanity with the heart of God." The Spirit of the Lord also said, speaking of Jesus, "I did everything I could for you while I was there, now do everything you can for me while you are there." My prayer is that this book will touch your heart and begin the journey God wants to take you on.

Chapter 2

Spoken in My Spirit

From My Journal

December 29, 2001

Words from my Father

I have invested in you, Mary Ann, and I am jealous and protective of that investment. I must allow you to die (to self) just as I had to allow my Son to die and accomplish my plan.

Though the pain is great, the Glory at "your" end is greater. As I have told you before, "At the end of you, there is Me." What I want you to be is my reflector. My reflector must be always in line with me!

I will allow you to see things, as I've said, some you

won't like. You must realize THIS IS NOT A GAME. I need you and I'm counting on you. Just as the moon is a reflector of the sun, you are to be a reflector of me. The moon does not question, it just does. (Matthew 5:16, 2 Corinthians 4:6-7)

You have cried out for my love, and you have it. I also have cried out for your love and must know that I have it. I will know that I have it as you turn your face more and more toward me and I see MY reflection in your face. What I give, I don't take back, and what you give me you must not take back. IT IS A COVENANT!!

The times you are feeling lonely, they are just feelings. How could I ever leave my reflector?! I am more with you than you are with yourself. There is only one thing that can come between you and me and that is SIN. I cannot look upon sin, and while I'm not looking at you, you cannot reflect me.

Warmth draws, cold repels. Warmth causes a person to lay prostrate and bask in it. Cold causes a person to coil up and hide. I want the warmth of my love reflecting off you to cause people to "Bask in me."

Just as you must be born again in Jesus, Jesus must be born again in you. To be born is to come into existence. Jesus came into existence into this world earth through the womb of his mother, as did you. Your trust and belief in Him cause your eternal existence WITH the Father. This is a spiritual thing. You must be born again "IN HIM," and He must be born again "in you." Again, it is a spiritual thing. Your mind may not understand, but "your spirit knows."

I will not allow you to place your trust in man for man is evil by nature. I tell you the truth, Mary Ann, I will control your every thought and deed. (A strong voice in my spirit. I am experiencing shaking and a knowing in my spirit; weeping and speaking in tongues.)

You have offered yourself to me, and I have accepted. You belong to me now. I am yours. and you are mine. (I felt like this was God the Father speaking to me. "Father, I turn from the cold of sin and turn to the warmth of your love.")

Do not lust after what belongs to another. Lust of the flesh would be your downfall. If I provide for others, do you not think I can and will provide for my reflector? Do not become drawn up into that state of "confused thinking." It is a mockery that angers me.

I am looking for someone who will just "simply believe in me" To believe is to trust and expect that I will do what I say I will do. REMEMBER, I spoke this to you, "BELIEVEING is knowing that my word is true. FAITH is believing that my word is for you. Your believing and your faith equal Trust in Me. That equation pleases me.

Do not fear, all things shall be revealed to you in my timing. Rest knowing that "I know." When I speak it to you, I want you to write it out. The written word shall be here for ages to come. The words you write will still be here when Jesus returns.

Keep your mind clean and listen to the things I

have to say. Remember "Garbage in; garbage out." I want, "My words in; my words out!"

I am the Most High God. Nothing, no-thing gets by me. Be it of me or not of me, I see it all.

December 31, 2001 - 2:45 a.m.

I awoke this a.m. and said, "What time is it, Lord?" I heard Him in my spirit clearly say, "It doesn't matter. Time is mine and you are in it. The clock is only for your point of reference, and it doesn't compare to mine. Everything is according to my plan, and you are beginning to see the mighty hand of God at work in many lives as I begin to move things around. Be still and watch what I do."

The things of the Spirit are real. The things of this natural world that man can see, and therefore thinks are real, are only temporary and fleeting at best.

The Spiritual world, the one I'm in sayeth God is real. That is the world I'm calling you to. As was told to you by my Prophetess (Diane), "I am pulling you behind the veil with me. Let go and take hold. Lose one and gain the other. I promise you (vow, covenant) you will never be sorry."

December 31st, 2001 - 3:47 a.m.

"I have just breathed MY LIFE into you," said the Lord. (Inside my spirit, Father God speaking.) "I breathe the breath of life into all mankind, but I have breathed into you, and you are truly blessed." At that very moment, "instant," quicker even than a moment, a breath filled me with a jerk. It was not a hiccup, it was unique; hard to explain, but I felt it, and I know it was God. Later this morning while searching scripture to confirm, I said, "Oh God, I love you." I could feel him smiling. "I love you too, my child. Keep going (searching)."

Oh, Heavenly Father, I have searched for a father all my life, and you've been there all the time. Oh, how I love you, and I kiss the face of God. I have touched heaven, and heaven has touched me.

While thinking about one of my grandchildren the Lord spoke clearly to me. "Your transformation will not be complete; you will never be like Jesus until, and unless, you love "all" without having "favorites." I didn't say anything about "like." I have already shown you the difference. I am training you in 'love.'"

"You have cried out for me to use you, and I will, but how can you do something you don't even understand? Jesus understood his mission, and He fulfilled it. So many of my people don't, but you will. The reason is you have been called, and you have chosen. Therefore, you are one of my called and chosen."

A word given to me at We Are One Ministry. (Her name was Janet or Janice; I don't remember which.) "You will see with the Eyes of God." I heard in my spirit, "The eyes of God are spiritual." I thought, Oh God, thank you! I was wondering what it meant.

Chapter 3

What is Love?

It seems like I've been chasing it all my life, and I would venture to say most of you have too. When I think I've got it, "it" is gone! That warm fuzzy feeling, where did it go? What we consider love is mostly lust, and lust must be fed constantly.

Love is a "living" force—a force so strong that it creates and also gives. Love is an action word, never passive. If felt in a passive way, it is not love.

It was love that caused God to move. God created man in his own image, and with his own breath gave life to man. I would say that's far from passive, wouldn't you? God's desire was to fellowship and exchange love with his creation, and he did just that until the thief came to steal, kill, and destroy all that God loves.

The thief only comes to steal and kill and destroy...

- John 10:10 (NIV)

Satan came in, and with the fall of man, God was separated from the creation of His love. Yes, the creation of His love, not the love of His creation. He has love for his creation, but it was the creation of his love.

Remember, "LOVE" is an action word, and "IT" has power. In fact, love is not just a word; it is a "LIVING FORCE!" The Bible assures us that God is "love," and what a mighty force He is!

When man fell in the garden, God gave the Son of His love to regain back to himself what that fall cost. It cost Him His relationship, so the Bible tells us in John 3:16 that God so loved the world that He gave His only begotten son.

We can all judge the depth of our love by how much we are willing to give. It is in our giving that we will receive. If everyone gives, everyone will eventually receive.

The world explains it this way, "What goes around, comes around." But God calls it "seed time and harvest." It is an old principle, as old as the Old Testament, yet as new as today. Plant it, and you "will" harvest it, whatever the "IT" is. There is life in the seed, and it must produce after its own kind.

God never changes, and His laws never change. The

word of God says, "Give and it shall...," not maybe, not might, but it "shall" be given.

The world is filled with all kinds of people, and they are, for the most part, "givers or takers." I'm quite sure we can all think of those who fit into each category, and at times, we've all probably been in each one.

I believe God wants us to be a little of both. Don't be shocked by that. Just think about it for a minute: a little giving and a little taking. That way, we all partake!

Satan would love to keep us confused about it, convincing some to give, give, give, not allowing ourselves to receive, and others to take, take, take, afraid to give anything of ourselves. Both are states of fear, and fear is clearly not of God. God is a God of order, and giving and receiving love certainly puts things in order.

I, for one, am learning, albeit at times ever so slowly, that when you are walking in love, there is that feeling of sweet peace. It is a feeling you can't quite explain. It's just there. You can't explain it because it's from God, and who can explain him?

Try to remember the first time you fell "in love." Relive it for a moment. You were at peace with the world. You wanted to give all you had and, at the same time, receive all the other person would give you.

God wants the same relationship with you and me. He has and will give us all He has. But you know, God is no respecter of persons, not even of himself. He wants you to give Him all of you in exchange for all of Him.

Give Him your sorrow for His joy. Give Him all your suffering for healing. Give Him your broken heart for a brand new one. But above all, give him your love. He, in return, will give you all His.

Try Him and see if He will not always "outgive you!" I promise you that you will never again have to ask,

"WHAT IS LOVE, AND WHERE CAN I GET IT?"

God is love and will give as much of Himself as you want. His limits are not in his giving; they are in our receiving.

> But the fruit of the Spirit is love, joy, peace, long-suffering, gentleness, goodness, faith, meekness, temperance: against such there is no law.
>
> - Galatians 5:22-23

Love is the first fruit of the Spirit, and the more fruit we produce, the more like Christ we become.

Jesus, the son of God, is perfect in every way, and it is God's desire that we become more and more like the Son of His love.

Love bears all things.

Believes all things.

Hopes all things.

Endures all things.

Love never fails.

Love suffers long and is kind; love does not envy; love does not parade itself, is not puffed up; does not behave rudely, does not seek its own, is not provoked, thinks no evil; does not rejoice in iniquity, but rejoices in the truth; bears all things, believes all things, hopes all things, endures all things. Love never fails.

- 1 Corinthians 13:4-8 (NKJV)

Chapter 4

Only My Love
In You

Dedicated to all the people who struggle with life and are dealing with the cares of this world, trying to love and be loved. All of you who are thinking, "One day, I will be able to love all people at all times." I venture to say that on your own, you cannot, but with the love of God on the inside of us, we all can.

At a time when I was feeling great pain, a pain of dying inside (feelings ranging from sadness to rage to fear), the Holy Spirit spoke, and as he spoke, I understood that experience was necessary. The Lord began by saying, "Your love must die so that you become able to carry the love of God." Satan's goal is to paralyze us with feelings I have just described. There is no love in him, and his desire is that we have none in us.

Dying to ourselves is painful. This all began when

the Lord spoke in my spirit, saying, "I am calling you into a ministry of love." I said, "Lord, I can't do it." That is when he began coaching me in a gentle voice. "You will not love them with your love; you will love them with mine."

The Lord began the process of showing me that it is not possible to love in the carnal, conditional type of love expressed by humanity (conditioned and tainted by the sins of this world) and, at the same time, love with the pure Agape love of God. For the love of Jesus to flow in and through us, we must first get out of the way. His desire is that we become empty, dead if you will, to ourselves and filled with Him. The Lord explains this in James 3:11. *"Does a spring send forth fresh water and bitter water from the same opening?"*

The anointing to carry the love of Jesus is a wonderful and, at the same time, costly calling. As Katherine Kuhlman said, "It will cost you everything." It will cost you the judgmental attitudes you may have and jealousies of others. It will cost you the fear of what others say about you or things they've done to you. Proverbs 29:25 says, *"The fear of man brings a snare, but whoever trusts in the Lord shall be safe."* (NKJV) Those things do not matter in God's plan. For Jesus to do what He came to do, those things could not matter. He had to keep His eyes and His feelings (and He had them) on his Father and the plan for His life. We see it clearly in John 6:38. *"For I have come down from heaven, not to do my own will, but of Him who sent me."* (NKJV)

I heard the Lord speak in my spirit, "You must first realize how much I love you. It is not about how much you do, or do not, love you, but how unconditionally I love you. Then you must lay down your life for Jesus and let Jesus come alive in you."

Every call of God has a price tag. "Are you willing to pay the price?" the Lord asked me. He then said, "I have called many, but few are chosen because few choose to be chosen, and of course, the choice is yours. Also, know this: I will not ask you to do anything alone. I want you to know that the rewards are magnificent, and what I begin in you, I will finish." The promise comes in Romans 9:28. *"For he will finish the work and cut it short in righteousness: because a short work will the LORD make upon the earth."*

"Do not concern yourself about past mistakes and failures. I am looking for willing and yielded vessels. I knew you and all your human failures, yet I loved you, and have called you."

Before I formed you in the womb., I knew you...
- Jeremiah 1:5 (NKJV)

In my spirit, I heard the Lord say, "After the vapor of your life is gone, what have you left of any value? The love you have lavished on and deposited into people I have placed in your path is the only lasting thing of value you can leave behind." Love is a gift to be freely given and freely received. It cannot be bought or sold. Our Heavenly Father loved us so much that he gave us

Jesus, His love wrapped up in flesh. Jesus was freely given and must be freely received.

The things of this world come and go, but the love of God is a constant, never-changing, never-ending force. Love is a force so strong that it is what will bring Jesus back. The Lord spoke in my spirit, "It will take a mighty and powerful force in these last days to bring in the lost souls and also bring Jesus back for the Church." The force he is talking about is LOVE, the Agape love of God, active and alive in His people. There is no greater force in Heaven or on Earth. God so loved the world that he gave all He had to redeem it. It is his love wrapped in human flesh, Jesus. The Bible tells us in John 3:16 just how much He loves us.

Love sent Jesus to the earth the first time, and it will bring Him back again. There is no more powerful force in all of Heaven than pure love. I heard in my spirit the Lord say, "When the power of love on this earth matches up with the love that sent Jesus, it will also bring Jesus back." Jesus is not coming back for a dirty bride (church), but one without spot or blemish.

> *That he might present it to himself a glorious church, not having spot, or wrinkle, or any such thing; but that it should be holy and without blemish.*
>
> - Ephesians 5:27

The kind of love Jesus had is the only thing that

will cause anyone to lose themselves and guide others in love to Jesus, the hope of our salvation. Jesus told us, "The things I do, you will do also."

Begin to make your own search for the way Jesus lived. He lived a life of simplicity but not one of poverty, for he had everything, and the wonderful thing is, he left it all here for you and me. Look for the things he did. He walked in love and peace, was humble, and yet had great strength. His strength was in knowing who he was and what he was to do. He did nothing without the Father. John 10:30 says, *"I and My Father are one."* We will get our strength the same way Jesus did.

> *Verily, verily, I say unto you, He that believeth on me, the works that I do shall he do also; and greater works than these shall he do; because I go unto my Father.*
>
> - John 14:12

Didn't Jesus love this world with the most selfless love this world has ever known? He lived his life as an example for us. He took all our sins upon himself. He then paid for that sin with his life at Calvary. He still loves us enough to send the Holy Spirit back to fill the void he left in us. The unfailing love Jesus had for God's fallen man is beyond our carnal comprehension. I do not believe we will fully understand until we see

Jesus face to face one day, and what a day that will be! The day we can sit and listen to him speak to us about the love that sent him willingly to that cross on Calvary.

Chapter 5

The Promise of
the Spirit

*If you love Me, keep My commandments. And I
will pray the Father, and He will give you
another Helper, that He may abide with you
forever—the Spirit of truth, whom the world
cannot receive, because it neither sees Him nor
knows Him; but you know Him, for He dwells
with you and will be in you. I will not leave you
orphans; I will come to you.*

- John 14:15-18 (NKJV)

Can we even begin to comprehend a love so strong
that after suffering death, hell, and the grave, a
man would still love you enough to send a replace-
ment for himself to care for you in his absence? When

the Lord Jesus took his sacrifice, his own blood, to the Father to atone for our sins, his love could not leave us alone without a comforter. Oh, that everyone the Lord places in our path will be able to remember the love we had for them after we are gone. The Lord said, "Be an example, a vessel so full of love that people will come to Jesus."

He said, "It is not easy, and death is painful. Jesus had to die, and you will have to die that I can live in and love through you." You must have faith in God in all things, and faith works in love. God wants us to have enough trust, which is faith, in the love that he has for us to know without a doubt that he will not leave us alone while we are learning to die to ourselves and become vessels he needs to carry the End Time anointing, which I believe is love. We are to love all of God's creation, not as we would, but as He does, seeing them through the blood of Jesus. Looking through the blood removes all their sin and yours. In doing this, you will touch God, and he will touch you. God has shown me that touching people with his love touches him.

I asked the Lord, "What will I do for you in eternity? He answered, "You will minister to my heart." I said, "How can I minister to the heart of almighty God?" He said, "My people are my heart."

The Lord has shown me that when we, his church (a called out, set apart, sanctified people), have touched the world with the agape love of God, Jesus will return. No one knows when that day is, but I believe we can hasten his return or delay it because the Lord said he would not have anyone perish.

> *The Lord is not slow in keeping his promise, as some understand slowness. Instead he is patient with you, not wanting anyone to perish, but everyone to come to repentance.*

- 2 Peter 3:9 (NIV)

Shouldn't everyone have at least one opportunity to experience the love of Jesus and receive him as their personal savior? I find it hard to believe that anyone experiencing the true agape love of God being witnessed before them would turn it down.

Most of us would give anything for true love. We long for it, crave it to the depths of our soul. We pray for it, cry for it, and chase after it in every way known to man. But God has shown me that it is like grabbing and reaching for a shadow. When I run, it runs. Life as we know it is fleeting, only a vapor. It is here for a short while and then gone, but the love of God is eternal.

A few months ago, while listening to the Holy Spirit, I heard him say, "When God pours out the anointing to carry his love, shame on you if you do not catch it, for it is God's end-time ministry." I heard this in my spirit: "Lose sight of yourself in the natural and let your life take on the image of Jesus. Purpose in your heart to let others see Jesus in you."

Jesus said in John 12:32, "*And I, if I be lifted up from the earth, will draw all men unto me.*" Have you ever felt anything that draws any stronger than love?

While talking to the Lord not long ago, I asked him, "Lord, if you love me, how much do you love me?" His answer was one of the most beautiful things I've ever heard. He said, "I love you to the depth and breadth of all that I am." All I could do was weep with a love I cannot explain.

God is no respecter of persons, so seek him and then ask the same question I asked. He will surely give you the same answer. It is the heart of God that we give our hearts and lives to him. In return, all that he has is ours. If you do not know Jesus as your personal savior, I pray you will come to know him today. I cannot imagine a day without his love.

A while ago, one of my daughters asked me, "Mom, do you believe the nails were placed in Jesus' hands or his wrists?" The person she had been talking to had said, "If they were in his hands, they would have ripped out because our hands are not that strong." In my spirit, I heard, "In his hands." Now, I can't prove this. I only know what the Bible says in John 20:27. "*Then He said to Thomas, 'Reach your finger here, and look at My hands; and reach your hand here, and put it into My side. Do not be unbelieving, but believing.'*" (NKJV)

I heard in my spirit, "The reason they did not tear

out was because Jesus did not struggle. He willingly hung there for you and me. It was not the nails that held him to that cross. It was his great love for you and for me that held him there." LOVE, the mightiest force in the world, held Jesus to the cross.

Chapter 6

Love, A Fruit of the Spirit

L ove in the natural can be and often is conditional. We say things like, "I will and do love you if you say and do the things I want." Or, "I love you if you do not make me angry or upset me in any way." This is a painful but familiar way almost all of us love most of the time. I regret to say that includes me. It is wrong because Jesus said to love those who hurt and despitefully use you.

(Jesus speaking) *"You have heard that it was said, 'You shall love your neighbor and hate your enemy.' But I say to you, love your enemies, bless those who curse you, do good to those who hate you, and pray for those who spitefully use you and persecute you, that you may be sons of your Father in heaven; for He makes His sun rise on the evil and on the good, and sends rain on the just and on the unjust."*

- Matthew 5:43-45 (NKJV)

In Galatians 5:22, we read that love is a fruit of the Spirit. I have tried the Agape God kind of love for the people I love and the ones I do not love. I believe it to be one of the hardest things to do on a consistent basis. But we must remember we serve a consistent, loving, and never-changing God who is changing us from glory to glory to become more like him. This kind of love is impossible on our own. If we could love perfectly apart from God, we would not need him, and it is his plan that we need him in everything!

The Bible has the perfect explanation of love in 1 Corinthians 13:4-8, and I try to pray daily, "Father, thank you that you are helping me walk in the first fruit of the Spirit. I cannot do it on my own, but in Jesus' name, I can." I am learning from the Bible that I can do all things through Christ.

Love suffers long and is kind; love does not envy; love does not parade itself, is not puffed up; does not behave rudely, does not seek its own, is not pro-voked, thinks no evil; does not rejoice in iniquity, but rejoices in the truth; bears all things, believes all things, hopes all things, endures all things. Love never fails.

- 1 Corinthians 13:4-8 (NKJV)

I do not know why God has called me into a ministry of love because all my life, I have struggled with the feelings of not being loved and the anger those feelings cause.

So, when God told me, "I have called you into a ministry of love." I said, "You what?! I can't do that, Lord, because I hate everybody." (That is no longer true, by the way.) In my spirit, I saw God smile, and he said, "You are not going to love them with your love. You're going to love them with mine."

The Holy Spirit spoke to me in my spirit. (Yes, He really does talk to us!) He said, "Those feelings are just that, feelings." No matter how people treat you or me, Jesus loves us, and that is what we are supposed to know and trust in.

I have found that anger is a cover and is easier (I thought) to deal with than the pain of feeling unloved. Anger is a lie and a pit of destruction that Satan wants us to fall into. Anger is a mighty destructive force. It rips apart all that gets in its way. The pain inside, deep pain that cannot be explained or even thought about anymore, like a meal, feeds the anger that, at times, is more alive than you are!

Anger is the thief that robs its victim of the blessings God has for your life. When that happens, the fruit of the Spirit is no longer a part of your life. You have lost all your joy; you do not or cannot love. You are too angry to love anyone. Peace of mind is out of the question, and who could even think about long-suffering. You do not have time for that; you are too angry and have been suffering all your life. Meekness is long gone. Goodness, "Is there any?" you wonder. Gentleness, you have given all yours away, and people only mistake it for weakness. Faith, "In what?!" you say. Temperance, or any control of self, was lost when you lost your "SELF" in the pain and abuse.

There is abuse inflicted by others and abuse inflicted by self because that has become comfortable. How do I know these things? I know them because the fact is, I, like so many others, have lived them.

To be a victim is to become a victimizer, even of yourself. People tire of things, and they tire of you. They move on, but by then, you have become so comfortable with the pain that you are uncomfortable without it. You diligently, yet unknowingly, look for your next pain inflictor, and they are easy to find because they are looking for you. The cycle begins...pain and anger, then anger and pain. Anger's best friend, Hatred, comes to join in. Anger has eaten up all the love, and the vacuum must be filled. Hatred and all her ugliness run right in.

What a gruesome pair, Anger and Hatred. The victim doesn't stand a chance. The victimizer doesn't stand a chance either, for that matter. Anger and hatred are sent in straight from hell and will destroy all that get in their way. Satan's plan is to kill you, steal from you, and destroy you. Anger and hatred are two of his most powerful warriors. Living like the devil, swapping blows with everyone does no good. You see, the people are not your enemy. The enemy is Satan, and he uses anyone he can.

Jesus knew the truth, and in Matthew 5:39, He said if a man strikes you, do not strike him back. That must put the enemy into confusion. Can you see Anger and Hatred doing that? No, they will tear your head off and eat it for lunch. Most victims realize at an early age, or at least I did, that anger hurts much less than the pain of not feeling loved. While angry, you are not aware of the pain, so you choose to be angry rather than feel the pain of physical, sexual, or verbal abuse or neglect of any kind. It is the lie Satan wants us to believe. The problem is, Anger and Hatred are just the blankets that cover up what is really going on. Jesus said in Matthew 5:44 to love your enemies. The sad thing about hatred and anger is they consume you, and that is Satan's plan. His plan is that you love no one. Believe me when I tell you that inside anger and hatred, and they do go hand in hand, there are no doors or windows. There is seemingly no way out.

Satan has you right where he wants you, he thinks! He has blinded you to everything on the outside. Please remember, though, that Satan will never create a situation from which God does not have an escape. Jesus, the son of God, is the doorway of our escape. He is our only way out. He is the example of "Do unto others as you would have them do unto you."

Let me stop right here and say that we will never succeed without God's instruction manual, the Bible. Outside of it is our destruction. Inside of it is our salvation. The Bible promises this in I Corinthians 10:13. Our escape is the mercy, grace, and agape love of God the Father, who has no favorites. He loves us in our sins, and He loves those who sin against us. All have sinned against him.

No temptation has overtaken you except such as is common to man; but God is faithful, who will not allow you to be tempted beyond what you are able, but with the temptation will also make the way of escape, that you may be able to bear it.

- 1 Corinthians 10:13 (NKJV)

When we get a real clear revelation of what Jesus on the cross did for each of us, we can weep not only for ourselves but for all of humanity. None of us are above being used by Satan unless we stay in the word (the Bible), prayed up, and so full of the Holy Spirit that there is not even a crack for Satan to enter. While in the wilderness, being tempted by Satan, Jesus defeated him with the word.

Everyone wants to receive love, but not everyone can give love. Your heart must be right. It cannot harbor envy, jealousy, or hardness of heart of any kind. Those things are sin, and sin will block true love. Remember, God is love, and God will be blocked from your life. The God kind of love is what we are all searching for. Many of us just do not realize what God's love is, so we spend our lives trying to fill that place in our hearts with wrong things and wrong people. It does not and will not ever work because God intended that place in our lives for himself. We belong to God, and he loves us unconditionally. He wants the same unconditional love from us for him, for ourselves, and for others.

On October 20, 1997, God began to speak to me as only He can. I attended and graduated from the School of Ministry at Abundant Life Christian Center in LaMarque, Texas, founded by Pastor Walter Hallum, a warm and Godly man I consider one of God's generals. While studying for a scripture test, the Lord gave me a message. I know it was God by the Holy Spirit because I was holding my Bible, and as he spoke, I began to weep.

This is the message the Lord gave me:

I want you to know that love not only needs a giver, but it also needs a receiver. Without a receiver, the giver is not necessary. This is what I am looking for in you...that you let me be necessary in your life. Until you know that, you know nothing.

For me, that was a "Thus sayeth the Lord!" I pray I never forget it.

The Lord made it plain that he wants to abide in me, and I abide in him. The same is true for you because Jesus tells us in John 15:4-5 to abide in him or we can do nothing. To abide in Jesus and have him abide in you, there must be love. Remember, God is love, and Jesus is God's son. If you do not love someone, you do not want to be with them, much less be in them and have them in you, spiritually speaking, that is. Jesus not only loved us enough to die for us, he loved us enough to live for us and with us through his word and example. God loved us so much that he planted his son Jesus so he could reap a harvest of love. Can you imagine the happiness in the heart of God when gardens of love spring up all over the world?! Don't you think that is why love is the first fruit of the Spirit?! I have given it a lot of thought, and I believe love was and is that important to God, and I wonder why we don't take it as seriously as He does. You must plant seeds of love to harvest a garden of love. Keep your eyes on the Gardener (God), not the garden (person). Remember, there is a growth process, and a harvest will always come. The garden is never greater than the Gardener. God will never allow anything to be more important to us than he is, and we should always keep that uppermost in our minds.

Just as bad seed bears bad fruit, no seed bears

no fruit. God will not prosper bad fruit, nor can he prosper no fruit. God is an action God, so set out today to love someone, and begin with yourself. You are someone, and you deserve to be loved. Like all seeds, we must remember there is a growth process, and it takes time to reap the harvest. Our spiritual gardens are like natural gardens. Some of them grow faster, while some of them just naturally grow slower. Your garden will need weeding and pruning. To live a life of love you will have to give up some things, like selfish desires and taking what you want when you want it, because left to grow wild, they will destroy your garden. But praise God, no one can prune your garden like he can. Are you getting your seed from the Kingdom of Heaven or the pit of hell?

If the Lord is your gardener, you will reap love because you will reap what you sow. You must decide what you want to grow. Do not plant anger, fear, and jealousy, and expect to grow love. Wouldn't our lives be greatly improved if we all walked in love? We must not become anxious and dig up our garden. Things of the flesh can cause us to give up and look for a new garden. Instead, ask the Lord to help you water your garden with love.

Fear is the root of the problem most of the time. Satan is the author of the problem, while Jesus is the author of the solution. Therefore, we must combat fear with love. We must strive to act like Jesus did. He looked through our faults and saw our needs. What a sad day for us if Jesus had looked at what we deserved. Thank God his heart was filled with love and compassion as he looked down through time, saw you and me, knowing we needed a savior, a teacher, a guide, and said, "Yes. For them, I will do it." What a precious savior he is, and I pray you know him.

No matter how we feel or how it looks, it must be possible because God does not expect us to do something we cannot do. Speaking in my spirit, he said, "I will never ask you to do anything I have not already done." It does not make any difference if we believe it or not or if we like it or not; love is a choice, and no one can make the choice for us. We must learn to live in love and be led by love, or Satan will lead us. Satan is our enemy, and he will do anything, use anyone, to get you and me to step out of love and into anger and rage, jealousy, hate, and fear.

Our destiny is to be like Jesus, who went before us, choosing to walk in love. Should we choose to do any less? Jesus is God's love manifest in flesh. We have a choice to live in this world as if it's a throwaway society or choose to live a life of love, striving to see the potential of what love can bring out in ourselves and others. Love is the glue that binds us to each other and to God. The Bible promises that nothing can separate us from God's love; his love for us, and his Agape love in us. If we grow closer to God and let his love grow in us, love will naturally pour out on everyone around us.

I believe the Bible says what it means and means what it says. Everything is in its place for a reason, and the reason is you and me. The Bible is our instruction manual for a perfect life.

God had a very good reason for placing Love as the first fruit of the Spirit. I believe he knew if we could master love, then all the other fruit would fall into place. Just try to walk in unconditional love for one twenty-four-hour period. In our human nature, it is almost impossible. Before Jesus' crucifixion, while talking to his heavenly Father, he said, *"I have declared unto them thy name and will declare it; that the love wherewith thou hast loved me may be in them, and I in them."* [John 17:26] Seeing this passage, I could understand how it is possible God's people could walk in unconditional love. If God the Father loved Jesus with perfect love, and that love is in us, and Jesus is in us, then perfect love has to be in us. The love, of course, is hidden beneath the sinful nature we inherited from Adam when he fell for Satan's lies. But God always gives us a way out, as Jesus declared in the book of John. Jesus said, "I have overcome the world."

> *"These things I have spoken to you, that in Me you may have peace. In the world you will have tribulation; but be of good cheer, I have overcome the world."*
>
> - John 16:33 (NKJV)

Jesus is our savior, redeemer, and example. He

overcame, and with him, we will overcome. He lived in the same world we live in with the same temptations, humiliation, and ugliness we face daily, yet he chose to walk in love. I believe the key word here is "chose." He did not have to, yet he chose to walk in love, so much so that it led him to the cross in our place. You might say, "Well, that's right, but he was God." That's true; Jesus was one hundred percent God, and he was also one hundred percent man. If not, he could not have died in our place.

I sincerely believe when we master love, we will automatically be able to walk in the other eight fruits of the Spirit. Love opens the door to the other fruit, and I believe the other eight fruits support the first one...LOVE.

I have heard pastors and teachers say anything you preach or teach, you will surely be tested in, and I completely agree. Every day, I am tested in the fruit of the Spirit, and wouldn't you know, unconditional love is one of the hardest for me. You see, love makes you vulnerable, and being vulnerable can be painful. When people hurt you, and they eventually will, it is easier if you are not operating in love. At least, that is what you think, but the truth is the unconditional love that Jesus had for you and me enables us to look through everything else and choose to see only with love. God will not give us more than we can bear and will not ask us to do something we cannot do. Therefore, I know I will walk in all nine fruits of the Spirit one day. God does not respect one person more than another, so if I can do it, you can do it, too.

The Bible tells us God is not looking for vessels of gold or silver but willing vessels. If we come to God with a willing heart, I know he will fill our vessel with all his love—so much love that it will flow out to everyone he places in our path. God does not waste anything; you can be sure that if he gives you love, he wants you to share it. Begin today giving love away because you can never outgive God.

I learned the art of hating at an early age. I guarantee that when you cry yourself to sleep at night longing for love, yet not knowing what it really is, you learn to hate. You ask yourself, "Is love improper touching that comes to you in the night whispering, 'I'm doing this because I love you.'? Okay," you tell yourself, "Love must be my sexuality." But Satan, the artist of hate, paints a great picture of condemnation for you. The stage is set, and you are the "Star." I've spent many years being abused and then lashing out in pain. Even if it was just verbal, Satan never tells you that you can kill yourself and everyone around you with your tongue. He is never going to show you his "ammunition." Satan is your enemy, and you are in a war!

In a vision, I saw words going out from our mouths like a man with a machine gun. Satan would step in, causing the words to make a U-turn and kill with the bullets (words) we send out. By himself, Satan has no bullets. God has given us a weapon Satan cannot overcome, and that weapon is love. The picture may at times look bleak, and at times unbearable, yet if we keep seeking Jesus, God's light of love in this world, that light will displace the darkness. The love I am talking about is the Agape Love of God.

I have struggled with love all my life, and I cried out to him, "Lord, I don't even like these people! How am I going to love them?" In my spirit, the Lord spoke gently to me, "I didn't say you have to like them. I said you must love them." After he got my attention, he began to give me a revelation.

This is the revelation he gave me:

To like someone, you must share common interests with that other person. You enjoy their company and feel happy in their presence. Maybe you smile when you think about them. But, to love someone, you must totally abandon your feelings in favor of them. That is what Jesus did. Do you really think Jesus liked the men who spit on him, beat him unmercifully, cursed him, and then hung him on a cross to die? No, he didn't like them at all. He, however, did love them enough to pray, "Father, forgive them, for they do not know what they do," and then hang there and die for their sins.

That is the definition of love the Lord revealed to me, and if each of us loves that way, we will, at some point in our lives, be the recipient of the kind of love that is the abandonment of self in favor of someone else. I am still fighting the battle, and it is not easy, but it was not easy for Jesus. I think we tend to forget

Jesus was a man, human in every way, just like we are. He had feelings and was tempted, yet he was without sin. Although the battle is hard at times, it is comforting to know we have the victory in Jesus. He told us, "I have overcome the world."

Satan wants to rob us of our joy, our peace and happiness, even our very lives. We must remember who our enemy is. It is not one another. Satan is our enemy, and it is a spiritual battle that will never be won in the natural, fighting each other. Satan knows this very well, and his goal is to keep us from knowing it. He would love nothing more than to keep us busy destroying each other with what we perceive as "my faults and your faults." Again, our battle is not carnal but mighty through the pulling down of strongholds. To my understanding, a stronghold is anything Satan can keep us imprisoned in. Satan loves nothing more than to take God's people captive, but Jesus came to set the captives free. Let's all vow, "Jesus, your coming was not in vain!"

My prayer is that every day, you and I take a step closer to the love of Jesus for each other and a step away from the traps Satan would have us fall into.

Chapter 7

Alabaster Box

The Cost of the Oil

> *Then, six days before the Passover, Jesus came to Bethany, where Lazarus was who had been dead, whom He had raised from the dead. There they made Him a supper; and Martha served, but Lazarus was one of those who sat at the table with Him. Then Mary took a pound of very costly oil of spikenard, anointed the feet of Jesus, and wiped His feet with her hair. And the house was filled with the fragrance of the oil.*

- John 12:1-3 (NKJV)

There came unto him a woman having an alabaster box of very precious ointment, and poured it on his head, as he sat at meat.

- Matthew 26:7

How many times have we stumbled through tears and shame, looking for a place to run? I can feel what Mary, the woman in the Bible, was feeling, and I do not believe it was an unthought-out act on her part when she poured out her oil on Jesus. She had most likely been carrying her oil for some time, refusing to waste a drop. She had probably determined that she would pour it where it was needed and where it would serve a purpose.

Most likely, we are carrying our alabaster box with the oil of our tears from broken hearts, shame, pain, and failures, running from person to person and place to place, looking for a safe place to pour our oil. Many times, what we end up with is an empty box. I have done this and never found a safe place to pour my "oil," not until Jesus reached down and covered me with his love. It is a love so unconditional that it doesn't matter what I purchased it with.

Perhaps you have run to men, or women, to alcohol, drugs, or attempted suicide, all the while looking for a way out of what has filled your alabaster box.

Every trial and heartache will do one of two things.

1. It will cause you to run from Jesus, or
2. It will cause you to run to Jesus.

We can take our oil, pour it out on Jesus, and allow him to turn it into joy. I am finding that on my knees, wrapped safely in his love, I can pour out everything I have onto him.

When allowed to, Jesus will turn our pain into praise. It is praise that fills his nostrils and praise that he inhabits. The Bible tells us in the Book of John that he inhabits the praises of his people, and the woman in John chapter 12 is still praised to this day for what she did for Jesus.

Jesus is so loving he will give us what he wants us to give him.

Just remember, no one can come to Jesus for you because you alone know where you have been on those long, dark, hopeless days and nights, in the mire and the muck. Only you know the times when you were a prisoner of your circumstances.

The people there criticized the woman that day for not holding on to the "costly oil," the oil that represented all she stood for and all she had been through. It was worth a year's wages. To one man, it was all he saw. Many times, to this day, that is all that is seen. "How will it benefit me?" But to the woman that day, it was useful only for pouring out on Jesus.

I believe she knew Jesus was her last hope. Like myself and probably yourself, she had tried everything and not found anything of value for the box that represented her life. When she found Jesus, can't you just imagine, her joy was unspeakable! SHE HAD FOUND THE REAL PURPOSE FOR HER OIL! I believe it was true for that woman, and I also believe it is true for you and me. Don't you know she had run everywhere she could think of, looking for a place to pour out her pain? By the time she found Jesus, she was at the end of herself. She was at the end of her shame and at the end of caring what others thought about her. Jesus was her last hope, her last chance, and her last attempt to escape the pain that accompanied her every move. When she knelt before his feet and poured out on him with great abandon, not caring about anything or anyone, a miracle took place in her life. The "Master" himself touched her like she had never been touched before. To her, at that moment, there was no one else in the room except her and Jesus.

At some point in our lives, we must all come into that room saying, "Okay, it's you and me, Jesus. Lord, you are all I need, and I'm pouring it all out on you." There is a saying, "When the world gives you lemons, turn it into lemonade." I believe Jesus is telling us, "When the world gives you pain, give it to Me, and I will turn it into joy unspeakable!" Jesus has a relationship for you like no other. It will cost you everything in your treasure box, all the tears and pain, but when he touches you, the cost is forgotten. ONLY HIS TOUCH MATTERS! That is what Mary, the woman at Jesus' feet, realized that day, and she wasn't concerned with what anyone thought.

That is the place each one of us must come to, the place where only his touch matters. Nothing and no one else matters at all. Give your all to Jesus, for he gave his all, which truly cost him everything. It cost him his place for a while, his dignity, peace of mind. It cost him his very life. What Jesus was willing to "pour out" paid the price for what we could never buy, and it is spelled "L.O.V.E." Although the cost of every treasure box is different, it is also the same. It will cost you everything. No one knows the cost of the oil in your alabaster box. Maybe no one else sees the value, or they think it is too valuable to pour out. Jesus is waiting for you to pour it all out on him so he can fill you up with the oil he paid for: the oil of peace, joy, and true everlasting love. It is the fresh oil of the Holy Spirit.

Love is a simple yet powerful force. It gives, not looking at or for a return. Love can flow like a mighty river, but it can also become obstructed like a mighty dam. It depends on the container it is in. True love comes at a high price that cannot be bought or sold on this world's market, and the rewards do not come from this world. You might buy a little fun for a while, a friend, houses, land, and all the possessions you long for, but you cannot buy everlasting love because it has already been purchased for you. The love that bought your salvation, healing, happiness, prosperity, and everything you will ever need was "FREELY GIVEN AND POURED OUT." That is the force of love poured out like a mighty river. The force of that love has never stopped and never will be. You can have that same love flowing in your life, but consider the cost because it will cost you everything.

You will have to give up everything of a selfish nature. (So many times, I struggle there.) Give up everything Satan has used to keep you behind that stagnant dam. You will have to become like the woman with the oil. She took the lid off and poured it all out. I believe she knew it was not hers to begin with, and it does not belong to you and me either. You have probably paid a high price for that little box of oil, but that is because you are buying a counterfeit of this world. It is not love. It comes from Satan. And he has no love in him. What Satan has may look pretty, but it is an empty box. You will spend your life running around trying to fill it up. It will cost you everything, and you will end up with nothing. If you are going to spend all that you have to fill your alabaster box, why not spend it on the real thing? One may look pretty on the outside, but it is empty. The other may look rugged and worn like the cross, the man (Jesus) who hung there, but inside that rugged and unattractive box is the greatest love the world has ever known.

How much have you paid? In Jesus' day, it was worth a year's wages. Ask yourself, "Has the cost been worth the price?" If it came from this world, I can promise it wasn't. Stop today and pour everything into Jesus, and He, in return, will fill you with a love like you have never known. You will not be able to contain it, and it will flow from you like a mighty river. The world would have you waste your oil on all its traps, pouring out looking for love, peace, and joy from a system controlled by "the prince of this world." In case you didn't know, his name is Satan. If he can convince you to continue pouring out for him, you will have nothing left for Jesus, the true Prince, and our soon-coming King.

The one who loves most, gives most, and Jesus gave all he had. Satan, on the other hand, is a taker. To truly love much is not to take but to give. Ask yourself, "How much am I willing to give?" When you have the answer, you will then know the cost of your oil. IS IT WORTH ALL YOU HAVE, NOTHING OR SOMEWHERE IN BETWEEN?

Then ask yourself, "What am I going to do with it?" I suggest we do not keep it, and let it become stale, but rather, pour it out, and let it become a refreshing on someone else. There are laws set into place. Jesus said, "Do unto others as you would have them do unto you." Seed time and harvest; sow and reap.

The world says, "Like is drawn to like," "Birds of a feather flock together," and "The apple doesn't fall far from the tree." Personally, I like the way Jesus said it. *"Give, and it shall be given unto you."* (Luke 6:30). You can be sure that as you pour out your oil (love) on someone else, there will be oil (love) poured out on you. Begin to pour your first love out on Jesus. As he pours his love out on you, there won't be a box big enough to hold It, and that love will naturally pour all around you. You cannot outgive God. He says to try him and see if he will not pour out a blessing you cannot contain. I have tried him, and he is true.

Pour the contents of your Alabaster Box all out on Jesus. Allow it to be buried "with him," and a new you will be resurrected "in him."

Chapter 8

Dressmaking

Jesus, the Perfect Pattern

Original Creator - God the Father
The Pattern - Jesus
The Instructions - The Bible
The Seamstress - The Holy Spirit in You

Every garment has a designer. Included in the design are pattern pieces and instructions for assembly. My desire is to pattern myself to be so much like Jesus that people become Jesus-conscious in my presence. I have discovered that it is also God's will. In fact, it was his will and desire before it was mine. It is also God's desire to give us the desires of our hearts. God longs to fulfill our heart's desire because he is the one who placed the desire there in the first place. When you begin to fulfill "your" desires by seeking him, he will show you the way.

> *My little children, of whom I am again in travail until Christ be formed in you.*
>
> - Galatians 4:19 (ASV)

Our purpose in our journey as Christians on this earth is to become an exact copy of Jesus, God's only begotten son. God the Father has no need for millions of sinful "Adamses" running around throughout the earth, manifesting all that Hell has to offer; committing murder, incest, rape, theft; destroying all God created for good. It is time we became like our big brother Jesus and less like our destroyer Satan. We need to take on the commission from God to lead all to do the same thing. You might say, "But how do I do that? I want to, but I just can't seem to do it." Well, I believe God has shown me, and with his help, I will show you. First and most of all, get into the "Word."

I'm sure most of you know a little about dress-making. Everyone should know that you must have a pattern. Without a pattern, the dress probably won't fit. Now, men, don't lose interest in dressmaking because some of the most famous dress designers are men. Pause for a moment and consider the greatest designer (creator) of them all. He is God our Heavenly Father. Even God used a pattern. He used himself.

> *So God created man in his own image, in the image of God created he him; male and female created he them.*
>
> - Genesis 1:27

When you see a dress you like, you might say, "Well, I can't have the original, but if I can find a pattern, I can make one just like it." You search, pray, and begin to read the Bible. The light of revelation begins to shine in your spirit. Jesus is the original and the pattern. You buy the pattern and take the pieces out of the envelope, and as you spread them out on the material you have chosen, you say, "My, this is beautiful, but how do I put it together?" Well, don't you know God is our perfect designer, who does not give you a pattern without instructions? Take hold of your Bible and proclaim, "This is my instruction." It is brought to life by the Holy Spirit. Now, there are some things to consider; first, you do not want the material to shrink, so you must pre-wash it. Wash it in the water of the word. Second, you must get all the edges straight and press out all the wrinkles. The wrinkles represent the sin in your life. Bring it to the cross, and let the blood of Jesus press out every wrinkle.

That he might sanctify and cleanse it with the washing of water by the word, that he might present it to himself a glorious church, not having spot, or wrinkle, or any such thing; but that it should be holy and without blemish.

- Ephesians 5:26-27

Make sure you lay out the fruit of the Spirit on your material.

But the fruit of the Spirit is love, joy, peace, longsuffering, kindness, goodness, faithfulness, meekness, self-control. Against such there is no law.

- Galatians 5:22-23 (NKJV)

Then, you will want to lay out a heart for lost souls on your material. God has a heart for every lost soul, and Jesus died for lost souls.

For God so loved the world, that he gave his only begotten Son, that whosoever believeth in him should not perish, but have everlasting life.

- John 3:16

Next, lay out healing for the sick. Jesus took all our sickness.

And also lay out deliverance from oppression. Jesus took the oppression meant for us.

> *But he was wounded for our transgressions, he was bruised for our iniquities: the chastisement of our peace was upon him; and with his stripes we are healed.*
>
> Isaiah 53:5

Do not forget to lay out the largest piece of all, seeking our Heavenly Father's will. Jesus' greatest desire was to do His Father's will. The Bible clearly tells us this in the book of John.

> *For I have come down from heaven, not to do My own will, but the will of Him who sent Me.*
>
> - John 6:38

After placing all the pieces down and cutting them out, it is time to put them all together. You might say, "Oh Lord! How do I do that?" Well, let me tell you that you must use a very special thread that will not pull apart. It is strong yet pliable, pure, and everlasting. It is called Scarlet Thread. It is the very blood of Jesus, the spotless lamb.

The firstborn and only begotten Son of God, Jesus's blood must run through everything you say and do. It is the very blood of Jesus that bought the plan of redemption—your redemption from death, hell, and the grave. With the blood of Jesus, the curse of Adam's sin is broken in your life. His blood does not cover your sin; it washes it away. At his last Passover meal, before he was crucified, Jesus spoke to his disciples.

> Then He took the cup (filled with wine), and gave thanks, and gave it to them, saying, "Drink from it, all of you. For this is My blood of the new covenant, which is shed for many for the remission of sins."

- Matthew 6:27-28 (NKJV), comment added

Our Heavenly Father knew through Adam's sin we were all a mess. Our dresses are torn and tattered. They are useless to him and to us. But our Father looked down upon us with great love and compassion and said, "I will give them the perfect pattern. It will contain everything they need to turn that mess into the exact copy of my original, Jesus." The pattern is a gift. It was purchased at a very high price. A life for a life for you at Calvary, by the original, and his name is Jesus.

Therefore, as through one man's offense judgment came to all men, resulting in condemnation, even so through one Man's righteous act the free gift came to all men, resulting in justification of life.

- Romans 5:18

I pray you give your life to Jesus this day. Just tell Him right now, "Lord, I am a mess, but I want to become an exact copy of the original." When you do that, "Your" pattern is waiting.

Jesus is our High Priest, so clothe (dress) yourself in his righteousness. A place in Heaven has been prepared for you if you will take off the old dress of sin and put on the "beautiful dress of righteousness" found in Christ Jesus. Just as sure as the mercy seat was on the Ark of the Covenant, Jesus is on the throne of God. If you do not know my Lord and Savior Jesus, I pray that you come to know him right now.

Please pray:

Father, I have sinned. I ask you to forgive me. I believe Jesus is your son. I believe he died on the cross for my sins and rose again, and from this day forward, I will live my life for you. In Jesus name, Amen.

Nuggets of Wisdom

What you keep your eyes on is what you WILL become, so keep your eyes on Jesus. Satan can only come into the "dry" places. The washing by the water of the Word (Bible) keeps the blood wet. Without the washing of the Word, the blood dries where you are concerned. Satan can only operate in the dry places. Therefore, keep yourself saturated in God's Word.

Be very careful to aid the prophets of God. For in assisting them, you are assisting the Word of God. To harm a prophet is to hinder the Word of God, for he speaks through his prophets.

In a vision I had:

I saw people bound up with chains wrapped around them. When the blood of Jesus poured from him onto them, the chains fell to the ground, and the chains could not rise up through the blood to bind them again.

Chapter 9

Who's the Father of Your Baby?

On January 31, 2002, I began to hear the Lord speak to me in my spirit concerning things he tries to birth upon the earth in general and in our personal lives. When Moses was just a baby, Pharaoh ordered all babies under the age of two years to be killed. The Holy Spirit spoke, "It is the same in the spirit." The enemy wants every call of God in your life to die before the age of two. He prefers it to be aborted before birth, but before age two, it is too young and insecure to make it. Under age two, a toddler falls as much as he stands. After age two, he becomes independent and takes off on his own. Just sit back and watch the action of any two-year-old. The same is true of anything God wants to birth in you. The enemy wants it aborted. If you make it through labor and delivery, the enemy will cause you to be too tired and weak to care for it, and in walks "Crib Death." Begin now to pray and ask God to send "babysitters" he knows you can trust to help you care for your new baby. You can't trust just anyone and everyone, so be aware because Satan will send in a "good-looking" baby killer. Never underestimate your enemy. He has some good-looking packages. Just as you bathe your baby in the natural, you must bathe your spiritual baby. In other words, the vision God has given you: books, love ministry, deliverance, evangelism, or whatever God has given you. Bathe whatever God has given you in prayer and keep it oiled (anointed). A mother or caregiver almost always puts oil or lotion on the freshly bathed baby. Love the gift or vision God has given you. Watch over it and never neglect it. All living things die from neglect, so never neglect the vision God has given you. To neglect a vision grieves God. Reference: The man with the one talent as opposed to the men with 10 and 5, Matthew 25:14-30.

Naturally, just before the arrival of a new baby, a dear friend or loved one will give a shower to celebrate and help defer the cost of that new arrival. A select group will be invited because not everyone will celebrate with you or care for that matter. Some would even be filled with envy. Never forget that the enemy is real, and he is powerful. Also, never forget that your God is ALL powerful, and he is the "FATHER OF YOUR BABY." Your baby is not a bastard to be discarded as illegitimate and walked away from in shame. It is a seed planted there by Almighty God. Trust him to be there in the delivery room and then be there through every stage of development. God will even be there when the baby grows up and has a life of its own.

Remember, the baby was loaned to you for a while, but, it belongs to God. Trust him to take care of it and also of you!

Chapter 10

Labor and Delivery

At the time of conception, joy and excitement are in the air! A seed has been planted and has begun to grow. With the growing of that seed, there is much anticipation and even some concern. Will it be a boy or a girl? Will it be healthy? What will it look like? Will I be able to take care of it? Am I even equipped to do this? There are so many questions to be answered!

About the time you become so heavy it seems like you can't go on another day, labor begins! With every hour that goes by, the pain intensifies, and you cry out to everyone listening, "I can't take this another minute!" The doctors and nurses are coaching you, saying, "Push! It will soon be over, and when you look at your baby, you will forget the pain." May I say, "That is not true." You never forget that there was pain. It is just that pain is no longer a part of your life.

The birthing process is painful, but when it is over, you dress that baby, wrap it in a pink or blue blanket, and take it home. It never enters your mind to say, "Wait a minute. Let me wrap the pain up and take it home, too." No, you leave the pain behind. It is no longer a part of your life. It has served its purpose; you have been delivered.

Let me say right here that the delivery must be full and complete. Preceding the baby comes the breaking of the water, then the baby is delivered, and then the afterbirth must be delivered. For the mother to return to normal, everything must be delivered and cleaned up. There will be several post-delivery exams to ensure a healthy recovery. You do not want anything to go undetected that could cause infection or problems of any kind.

Wouldn't you know God designed it the same way in the spirit realm as in the natural realm? First comes the water; it is the washing of the water by the Word. Just as there is water for delivery in the natural, there must be "the water" in your spiritual delivery. The blood of Jesus washes us clean of all debris and anything left over from our sinful lives.

We must realize there are "legitimate babies" in our lives conceived by the Holy Spirit and our walk with Jesus, but there are also illegitimate babies" conceived with Satan.

In our walk with Jesus and the Holy Spirit, there is

salvation, prosperity, health, happiness, long life, and all the fruit of the Spirit. The Holy Spirit talks to us here, and Jesus talks to the Father for us in Heaven. How much better could things get than to have a Father, Son, and Holy Spirit involved in your life?

Walking with Satan, there is depression, drug and alcohol abuse, suicide, murder, and every wicked thing that can be conceived while sleeping with the enemy. But praise God; there is hope for us through the delivering power of Jesus' blood. I strongly suggest, if you have not given your heart to Jesus as your personal Savior, do it now, and let him cleanse, heal and deliver you.

It is very powerful, yet God made it so simple. Just believe that Jesus is the Son of God, that he died on the cross for your sins and rose again. Ask him to forgive you and become the Lord of your life. Confess it out loud to someone because Jesus said, "If you confess me before men, I will confess you before my Father." As soon as you've done that, the cleansing and delivery begin. WELCOME TO THE FAMILY OF GOD!

Chapter 11

The Tree

A tree is chosen. It has been growing for years; the builder and architect come along and choose this very tree because they can see it will fulfill their need. As it is cut down, stripped, cleansed, and shaped into many lengths, widths, and sizes, the tree does not know what is happening. It doesn't know why it's being changed and taken from the place it has always known. The builder and architect don't talk to the tree or explain why it is being cut up. But after being cut down and run through the lumber mill, where it is washed, cut, and left to dry, they all come back, pick up the pieces of the tree, and take it on a journey. Remember, the tree has only known the forest where it has been growing, so any distance is a journey.

On arriving at the destination chosen by the builder, not chosen by the tree, it is dropped off onto the ground. Strangers come and begin to handle the parts of the tree. These strangers have been sent by the builder unbeknownst to the tree. The tree still considers itself a tree even though it now looks nothing like a tree. These strangers have "tools," and they begin to hammer, saw, and bend. The sawing has left most of the tree as dust on the ground. The bending has put pressure unknown before, and, of course, the hammering has driven nails designed to keep it in place.

Partway into this operation a storm comes, and the workers leave as they do not work in the rain. Again, the tree is left alone to wonder, "Where am I, and why am I here? Does anyone know?" Then, one day, the sun (Son) shines through the clouds, and the workers all return. At the end of the scheduled time, they have each fulfilled their jobs. They put away their saws, hammers, and nails, not thinking about the tree. Then, in walks the builder and architect. They look around, walk through every room, and exclaim to each other, "What a beautiful, glorious, magnificent mansion this is! It is going to be a wonderful home for someone!"

This is not the end of the story for the tree. No, it is just the beginning. You see, it is just the first of many of its kind. The builder will use it as a model for the neighborhood he will build. His neighborhood will have many mansions, and this is just the first. The architect will send landscapers to dress up the grounds around the mansion and line the entrance with beautiful fragrant flowers. Invitations will go out for all to come and see the mansion. When word gets out that there is a beautiful mansion built from a tree, excitement builds, and all the trees stand tall, asking each other, "Do you think I could be used by the builder and turned into a mansion?" The Architect says, "Of course, you can, but you must allow yourself to be placed into the builder's hands."

Remember, on his own, the tree can never be anything but a tree, but in the Master Builder's hands, it can become a mansion!

I pray, "Help me, Lord, to become a mansion!"

Chapter 12

Esther

As was Esther, we all are placed here by God "for such a time as this." And as with her, there must be preparation time: a time of cleansing, purifying, and beautification inwardly, as well as outwardly. To accomplish God's call on our lives, we must have that sweet smell of confidence that we are prepared at any moment to answer the King's call. Remembering that we are a temple of the Holy Spirit, we are cleansed and polished "inwardly" having a reverence for, and full knowledge of, His word, and "outwardly" by caring for our bodies (our temple) with the bath of oils, creams, and perfumes.

As we see in the Book of Esther, it is biblical to care for our bodies. If you want to get anyone's attention, you must first "get" their attention, if you know what I mean. No one will come near you, much less give you their attention, if you have stinking thinking and, let's just say, an unpleasant outer temple.

Through His word, God will clean up the inner temple, and I will suggest how to improve the outer temple. Queen Esther had a pure heart and a love for her people, but she would not have gotten the king's attention had she not prepared what the king would see first. I believe the king was first attracted to Esther's outer beauty.

The time Esther was willing to spend preparing for what God needed her to do saved her and her people. To this day, the Jewish people celebrate this time.

Let us strive from now on to become modern-day Esthers. The Lord is calling each of us to get prepared and be prepared to lead our people out of bondage. It is not an overnight process; it takes much prayer and submission to the Holy Spirit working inside us. There will have to be separation and a willingness to be taken from the carnal life that has become so comfortable and familiar to the realm of the Spirit. In that realm, we are allowed to see and hear from God the Father just as Jesus did when he walked on this earth. He certainly heard from his Father and made a way, leading God's people out. He leads us all out of sin and death into forgiveness and eternal life. That was his call and his mission, and he fulfilled it.

What is your call and mission? Ask God to show you, and then allow yourself to be prepared.

Chapter 13

The Order of Things

God the Organizer

Jesus the Administrator

Holy Spirit the Manifester

Text References

The Organizer:

Genesis chapter One, "In the beginning God created..."

The Administrator:

John 14:21 (Jesus speaking), "I tell you the truth, anyone who has faith in me will..."

The Manifester:

John 16:14 (Jesus speaking of the Holy Spirit), "He will bring glory to me by taking from what is mine and making it known to you."

God is the Organizer

God is a God of order. Organization and order go hand in hand. He spoke all things into being. Can you just imagine what a universe we would have if God were a haphazard God? Creation would be total confusion.

In your mind's eye, try to paint this picture: instead of the wind at your back, you have it blowing up your skirt, so to speak. Can you see yourself in a scene like that?! Or perhaps gravity is holding you sometimes and at other times just letting you go. Can you see yourself putting a bite of food in your mouth today and tomorrow, God saying, "No, I want you to put it in your ear today." We laugh, and it's okay to laugh, but it's also serious. God created us in His image, and he desires us to be as dear children and imitate him. Therefore, he is calling us to be organized.

Jesus is the Administrator

The Administrator carries out the plans of the Organizer. He says to be disciples. A disciple is one who continues the work of the one who went before. Jesus, in essence, is saying, "Walk upon the earth doing the things I did. Do not carry out the things you want to do when you want to do them. Go to that person lying on their bed of affliction, lay hands on them, and pray. Go into the ghettos and palaces, preaching the acceptable year of the Lord. Tell the people I am their soon-coming King. Tell them to fall on their knees and look up. Tell them I died, but I have risen, and I AM coming back. Tell them I AM their hope in their darkest hour." These are the things Jesus did as the Administrator of the Organizer. "I did all my Father asked me to do. That was my calling, and I fulfilled it."

Holy Spirit is the Manifester

The Manifester has heard the call of the Organizer. He sees the Administrator always in obedience, moving on behalf of the Organizer. The Administrator is busy setting things in place and making sure the wishes of the Organizer are being carried out.

When everything is complete, the Manifester moves. Salvation is in place! When you call upon the Lord, the Holy Spirit moves, and salvation is manifested in your life. Healing is in place. Prayer goes up over your sick body, and healing is manifested. Discord may be stirring in your life and family situations, but the great Manifester is fast at work, bringing peace that passes all understanding.

Let us thank God today, and every day for that matter, that we are so blessed to be a people that can call ourselves "Children of the Most High God." Our mandate is to be imitators of Him.

Organize our lives according to his instructions.

Administrate the things in our life (set things into motion).

Manifest and reap the harvest of our good work.

For it is his good pleasure to bless "his dear children."

Chapter 14

Your Words

Text References

Hebrews 10:23 - God watches over His word to perform it.

Then Hebrews 11:3 – The entire world was formed at God's command.

I would like you to listen closely because I'm about to share a "Rhema" word given to me by the Holy Spirit. Holding up the Bible, I asked, "Who can tell me what this is?" We all know it is the Bible, but what is it really? IT IS WORD, God's word. They (God's words) created everything just the way he wanted it.

How many know Satan has no words: zip, zero, none! HE CANNOT create anything. But he knows God's word, and he listens to our words. But he HAS NO WORDS OF HIS OWN. Take note of that.

How often do we as women have someone ask, "How are you today?" We reply, "Oh, it's that curse! I have P.M.S., my head hurts, and I've been crying all day!" Or you men might respond, "I've worked all day, I'm tired, my children are sick, and I can't pay my bills!"

Well, did you know Jesus redeemed us from all those curses? Of course, you do! You've been taught the same thing over and over, so why, in the name of Jesus, are you still struggling?

Would you like to know what the Lord told me? It is simple yet so profound. Remember what I said in the beginning? This book, the Bible, is the word of God, and Satan has no words. All he can do is take God's words and pervert them. God's word is "Thus sayeth the Lord," not "Thus sayeth Satan!"

While crying out to God about something and "reminding" him about watching over his word, he "reminded" me that I was exactly right; he watches over his word. The Lord spoke to me in my spirit. He said, "Mary Ann, did you hear what you just said? I WATCH OVER MY WORD. Satan watches over "your words." And just as my words work for you, the words you give Satan, he uses against you." (This was the big revelation.)

This is what I saw in a vision. Please try to "see" it for yourself. God spoke out, and his words are still there, giving life. Every word he spoke is still there, giving life. EVERY WORD he spoke is still there. The same is true for yourself. See yourself speaking and the words flowing out in front of you forever. You will eventually walk into them. If they have been God's words, they are life for every area of your life, but if they have just been your words of doubt and unbelief, Satan is waiting to catch them and shoot you down. REMEMBER, he has no words of his own. In my vision, I saw Satan with a "Machine Gun" and myself feeding him endless "rounds" of ammunition to kill me with, but when I quit speaking, he ran out of ammo. I believe Satan is easily bored and confused. Since he is the father of lies, he won't speak God's word (the truth). So, when you and I quit speaking, he becomes bored and confused. During the boredom and confusion, he goes on to more exciting ground.

We here are leaders. We are chosen, and people will follow, so I extend a challenge to all of us to choose a partner, someone we will be honest with, and decide how we want to work it, but have an accountability system between us. For a month, put a mark down every time you speak something against what God says. I can promise you Satan is putting it down. At the end of a month's time, the "loser" takes the "winner" out to lunch or whatever you both have agreed on. Let's choose someone other than our spouse (man-man, woman-woman), and for now, let's keep it here.

This has brought excitement to my spirit, and I hope it will bring excitement to yours also.

As you can tell by reading this, I was teaching a class. At the time, I was teaching the mass choir of Gulf Meadows Church, Houston, Texas. The church pastor at the time was Pastor Roy Love. He is my pastor today (2023), by the way. He is a man of God I love and respect. He trusted me enough to minister to the choir. I believe this message is important enough to share with everyone, so choose a partner and get started! Let's send the devil packing!

Chapter 15

At the End
of You

While dealing with me on some things in my life and "my" way of judging things and people, the Lord said something to me that I pray has changed my life forever. He said, "There are two questions I will ask you at the end of your life. There will be many, but two important ones are: one, did you read my word? (I know you did.), and two, could you not hear me when I lay out all my examples before you?"

He said, "At the end of your life, and all your relationships, there is me. Did I not speak to you about how I have, and will, deal with every situation in every life? Your life is a journey. You are traveling from you to me. I am the Lord, and you are a part of my body. You must be willing to leave yourself and join me. I cannot leave my Father and join you in the nature of the world Satan is controlling, so you must leave the ties you have to this world and join me."

"While in the boat on the lake, did I not bid Peter, 'Come! Do not fear, for at the end of your fears, Peter, there is me.'? Think about Lazareth. At the end of his life, did I not call him forth? In the natural world, Lazareth was dead and buried. All hope was gone. But, in the end, was I not there to call him forth? At the end of Lazareth, there was me. How much more demonstration is needed for you to understand that at the end of you, there is me!"

"I am telling you to go and sin no more. Come when I call you forth to a life of my purpose, the life I created you for."

Epilogue

I pray that what I have shared with you will en-courage you to leave behind your fears, doubts, and anything else you can think of that would keep you from realizing how much God loves you, wants the best for you, and to the best of your ability, pass it on to everyone the Lord places in your path.

Prayer

Heavenly Father,

When I meet you face to face at the end of my life here on earth, my prayer is that I hear you say, "My child, you have loved me well."

Love is the ministry you called me to; it has not been easy, and at times, it has been unrecognizable. I have even fought against it. I recall the day you gave me the name of it, "HEART OF GOD MINISTRY." I said, "No, God, I hate everybody. I don't even like them!" In my spirit, you replied, "I didn't ask you to like them, but I did say, you will love them with my love."

As I travel farther along this path of life, Lord, I am truly grateful for what you called me to do. Father, please forgive me when I fail and keep encouraging me along the way. In Jesus name, I pray. Amen.

Message to the Reader

Dear reader,

Please know I no longer have feelings of hatred. The Lord has helped me along the way to forgive hurts and injustices. Our lives are made up of choices, and "I CHOOSE LOVE!"

November 29, 2023:

This struggle I had with the Lord was in the late 1990's. At the time of this writing, I am 84 years of age, and I can say, "With the constant help of my Savior, I have come a very long way!"

Notes

Notes

Notes

Notes

Notes

Notes

Notes

Notes

Notes

Notes

Notes

www.ingramcontent.com/pod-product-compliance
Lightning Source LLC
Chambersburg PA
CBHW060338130626
46553CB00003B/1047